Mary Cerciello is a prayer warrior and prophetic intercessor who has been given a gift of intimacy with her Holy Spirit, Messiah, and Abba Father. Her book, *Touching Heaven from the Empire State Building*, teaches us that through this gift of intimacy she has enjoyed many encounters with the Glory of her Most High God! This book brings to life these spiritual and prophetic experiences. For anyone seeking an intimate relationship with his or her Messiah or just knowing more in your search for the One and Only God, it is a must read! The words come forth and grab you, giving you an intense desire to experience a tremendous intimacy with the Creator of Heaven and Earth!

Dr. Charlie Kluge,
Rabbi, Gesher Shalom of the Palm Beaches, President of Gesher International Ministries, Inc. Past President of Messianic Jewish Alliance of America and Bernard Baruch B'nai B'rith.

Besides a direct encounter with the Lord Himself, there may be nothing as edifying as being in close contact with someone who has had a lifetime walk with Jesus, the manifest glory of God. I have every reason to believe that Mary Cerciello's accurate prophetic ministry is a result of her blessings in the glory manifestations, in the glory fellowships, in the glory encounters some of which I personally have been a blessed witness.

In this time of global harvesting, nothing will do but the glory of the Lord in the lives and ministries of the truly called. Read this book and your life will be so enriched, and thus enriched, you will be hungering after the glory outpouring: the presence of God in Jesus, the only key for a true effective ministry in the power of the Holy Spirit.

Archbishop Joseph Joel Laurore,
World Revival Temple, Tulsa, OK.

Mary Cerciello has the heart of a true marketplace pioneer and as I've watched her over the years, she has navigated many challenges with a strong commitment to the visionary principles God has set in her life. As she enters into greater understanding of God's Kingdom, she is finding a governmental depth that she's always embraced in the marketplace and business that is taking her into revelation of His greater glory to impact the world. Dr. Mary's book on "Glory Encounters" is a must read. You will be touched by His greater glory that emanates from each page.

Dr. Rick Kendall,
President Victory Ministries, Stuart, FL

This book is about imparting truth from the Spirit. By sharing these real-life encounters, Mary shares her heart. This lifestyle of worship will bring us to a place of true intimacy with the Lord. His presence brings healing, revelation, blessing, and so much more. I believe the reader will be encouraged and motivated to go deeper with God. May God bless the writer and the reader and may the Author and Finisher of our faith be with us all.

Dr. David Donnally,
President, Legacy Church Ministries, Lake Worth, FL

It is with joy that I recommend Mary Cerciello's testimonial concerning her walk with the Lord Jesus. In reading the book I was inspired to worship more, expect more, and receive more in the Lord's presence! I believe it will do the same for you. I found the book to be insightful and full of pithy teaching as Dr. Mary shares with us the joy that she has personally experienced as she enters the glorious presence of Jesus. I especially appreciate the fact that Dr. Mary shares with us the hardships that she has gone through in life, thus revealing to us that experiencing God's glorious presence doesn't shield us from the hardships of life, but instead empowers us to live victoriously through it all! Step into Dr. Mary's world with anticipation! You're going to enjoy it!

Dr. David Fleming,
Christ International Church, Miami, FL

Dr. Mary is a prolific writer. *Touching Heaven* is a timely book that will ignite the fire within and cause you to hunger for more. I recommend this book.

Dr. Sonia B. Elliott,
Eagle's Wings Ministries, Margate, FL

MARY CERCIELLO

TOUCHING HEAVEN FROM THE EMPIRE STATE BUILDING

Glory Encounters in Heavenly Places

PREFACE

As you read the chapters of this book you will come to understand that the Lord is no respecter of persons and that He will manifest His presence to you and through you in mighty and sometimes unusual ways. But first, as a believer in Christ, you need to have a passionate desire for His presence and His Word. Through the understanding that will come to you via praise and worship, you will come to know Him as the lover of your soul and as the Bride of Christ. In doing so, you will cease from your struggle about spiritual things. Through worship and the glory, you will understand the Glory Realm and begin to change as a fire rises up within you that transforms lives around you.

This book is about the Glory of God and how you can tap into heaven and experience His Glory presence. Each chapter concludes with an "Encounter with God" to help you take action on what is being shared. Learning to enter into His Glory will support you through some of the most difficult times of life.

The story takes place in New York City at the Prayer Tower located on the 68th floor of the Empire State Building as well as the Calvary Campgrounds in Ashland, VA. While I was under the ministries of Rev. Ruth Heflin and Rev. Gwendolin Sims Warren, you will read throughout the chapters, testimonials on a number of different encounters that I had with the Lord and seeing

His glory manifested. In addition, the insights in this book will mentor and teach you how to be a walking carrier of the Glory with influence.

In Hebrews 13:8 (NIV) it says, *"Jesus Christ is the same yesterday and today and forever."* What He did years ago, He can do the same today because he never changes. Come, the glory invites you into the supernatural realm. Jesus wants to show you more. Every invitation is an opportunity to see Him and to arise and shine.

With Love and Affection,
Dr. Mary Cerciello

CHAPTER ONE

UNUSUAL GLORY ENCOUNTER

John 14:6 (NIV) "I am the way and the truth and the life. No one comes to the Father except through me."

It was the mid 1980's in midtown Manhattan, NYC at a fellowship group when the Holy Spirit tugged at my heart. It was Rabbi Howie, a Messianic believer, who prayed with me to receive Yeshua, Jesus, as my personal Lord and Savior. My life made a sudden shift.

After spending several years as an actress, I finally found the Pearl of Great Price – Yeshua, Jesus. I was always searching for truth and the fulfillment and purpose of life as an actress. When I found Yeshua, I did not have to search any further because He filled that void in my life. Since that time an all-consuming fire burned within me. After finding the Truth, I left the acting profession to spend time with the Lord and explore other areas of business.

Before long, a new door of employment opened, and I was hired at the Helmsley Palace Hotel in midtown Manhattan. Leona and Harry Helmsley owned the Palace Hotel and a great deal of real estate in New York. They also owned the Empire State Building, the Pan Am building and much more. Leona was difficult with her employees. She demanded perfection; much like the boss depicted in the motion picture film, *The Devil Wears Prada.*

My job at the Palace was as liaison between sixty-five chefs and the banquet department. I reported directly to Chef Adrien, who was a very famous Chef from Paris.

During my lunch breaks, I would go under the stairwells of the hotel and intercede for an hour praying for the city. One afternoon, I came up from the stairwell and into the hotel kitchen. At that precise moment, my face felt like it was transformed, and Jesus's face replaced mine. I was experiencing something supernatural - Jesus was looking through my eyes and my face was transforming into his image as I approached the Sous Chef. When the Sous Chef looked at me with fear on his face, he said, "What is it?" I looked at him with a soft compassionate voice, "It's Jesus." Immediately, the Sous Chef, who was of Muslim decent, ran in fear into the gigantic freezer that was inside the kitchen. I felt a little nervous at that moment, but I trusted the Lord. I know the Lord was revealing Himself to the Sous Chef.

When Jesus and His glory are revealed the atmosphere changes, and those around you either see or sense the change. Thankfully, the Sous Chef did come out of the freezer but there was little communication thereafter.

That was my first encounter with Jesus working in my life in a supernatural way with signs and wonders. For example, in Exodus 34:30, when Moses came down from Mt. Sinai with the Tablets in his hand, his face was radiant. The Israelites saw him, and they feared to come near him.

I experienced the same manifestation of Jesus transforming and replacing my face to His, in front of Apostolic Church Leaders. They, too, saw Him and either looked away or scurried away. I understood what God was trying to accomplish through these encounters - He was revealing Himself to them.

Throughout the chapters of this book, you will read testimonials on a number of different encounters that I had with the Lord and His manifested glory. It is always God's heart to take you to different levels and to experience Him in special ways that are meaningful to you.

TRILOGY
PROFESSIONAL PUBLISHING MEETS POWERFUL PROMOTION
A wholly owned subsidiary of TBN

Touching Heaven from the Empire State Building

Trilogy Christian Publishers
A Wholly Owned Subsidiary of Trinity Broadcasting Network
2442 Michelle Drive
Tustin, CA 92780

Manufactured in the United States of America

10 9 8 7 6 5 4 3 2 1
Library of Congress Cataloging-in-Publication Data is available.
ISBN: 979-8-88738-249-4
ISBN: 979-8-88738-250-0

DEDICATION

With a grateful heart, this book is dedicated to my brother Joseph who recently passed to heaven. I celebrate your life.

ACKNOWLEDGEMENTS

Pastor Carol Fleming, Christ International Church, Miami, FL -- Thank you for your prayers, loving encouragement, and sound counsel.

Back to Jesus Movement Prayer Warriors, Miami, FL -- Special thanks to the prayer warriors who supported me in this endeavor.

Rev. Dr. Roxanne M. Mitchell, Pastor, Jerusalem AME Zion Church, Tuscaloosa, Alabama -- Special thanks for your support and assistance with the editing of this book.

Special thanks to the Prayer Tower warriors who labored in continuous prayer for New York City and the Nations: Ministers Gwen Deberry, Yvonne Reed, Jayne Skoog, Julio Vitolo, and Sonja Wilson.

TABLE OF CONTENTS

ENCOUNTERS WITH GOD

Jesus said in John 17:22, "I have given them the glory that you gave me, that they may be one as we are one."

We were born and designed to live in the Glory of God. Everyone washed in the blood of Jesus is invited into this interaction and glory. We were created to get answers to bring breakthrough to those around us. We were created to subdue darkness.

As a believer in Christ, if you live a life of prayer and seek after the things of God and allow the Holy Spirit free reign in your life, He will manifest His presence in numerous ways. He desires to be close to you. He wants you to encounter and reflect His glory.

Let us Pray: *Lord, I want to see your glory. I want to live in your glory and see lives healed and transformed for you. I want to be an active carrier of your glory.*

CHAPTER TWO

PRAYER TOWER - EMPIRE STATE BUILDING

Habakkuk 2:14 (NIV) "For the earth shall be filled with the knowledge of the glory of the Lord, as the waters cover the sea."

I would usually meet my friends Regina DeBoer and Roberta Sieber after work so we could pray and fellowship together. We were committed as young believers to pray diligently for Israel and the Nations. We were called as Intercessors by the Lord and forerunners in the City of New York to bring unity and fellowship to those who were new believers in Christ.

Regina was a successful textile businesswoman who lived in a large east side Manhattan apartment where she loved to entertain. Her apartment looked like a little Victorian palace. Roberta and her husband George were successful business owners and lived in the same area. Regina's gift of hospitality and cooking and Roberta's gift to draw people together, led them to invite Missionaries and Ministers to their homes when they visited NYC. They both frequently brought a group of businessmen and women together in their homes for fellowship and Bible study because there were few Evangelical churches in the city at that time. As young believers, we were full of zeal but needed to be grounded in God's Word.

The three of us would get together at least three times a week to fellowship and pray. Regina's textile business was located on the 68th floor of the Empire State Building. We called it the Prayer Tower since we frequently met there.

We were so hungry for God that we would travel to Bible conferences and camp meetings all over the U.S. when we were able. We were fortunate that George had access to a private plane and pilot. One of our favorite places was Calvary Campground in Ashland, Virginia. Calvary Campground was a place where missionaries went for rest and refreshment. *It was a revival center.* This is where we first met Rev. Ruth Ward Heflin.

During her lifetime, Sister Ruth has lived all over the world serving the Lord and ministering to the Nations. She preached to multitudes and ministered to kings and world leaders. Her ministry was noted for its prophetic anointing and revelation and her ability to lead people into worship.

She was born into a classic Pentecostal pastor's family where she eventually became the director at the Calvary

Pentecostal Campground, a worship and revival center located about an hour south of Washington, D.C.

Sister Ruth was later called to Jerusalem, Israel where she lived and ministered at her home, the Halcyon House. For twenty-five years, Jerusalem was her home where she received the nations for prayer and worship. The Lord told her, "You sow to the heavens, and I will sow to the earth." That was the way her ministry Mt. Zion Fellowship was born as an international prayer ministry in Jerusalem. Sister Ruth was a prophetess for the Nations.

I spent time in Jerusalem at the Halcyon House and toured the city with Sister Ruth and her team. At that time, she organized her "Pray for the Peace of Jerusalem Conference" at a hotel within the city which many people attended. We worshiped and prayed for the nations, and we were filled to overflowing by His Spirit.

In her book, Glory, *A Jerusalem Experience*, Sister Ruth wrote, "*What is the Glory? It is the realm of eternity. It is the revelation of the presence of God. He is Glory! As air is to the atmosphere of the Earth, so glory is the atmosphere of Heaven. Praise until the spirit of worship comes, worship until the glory comes. Then stand in the glory!*[1]"

Every time I was around Sister Ruth she spoke of the Glory and praying for the nations. She had a word for every nation she visited because the Glory *and knowledge of it,* covers the earth to mend it. This means it's the knowledge of knowing God, and the knowledge of His

Glory that lives within every believer to help others. It is also the knowledge of His Word and believing it and the knowledge of knowing who you are in Christ and demonstrating it by His Spirit.

Sister Ruth spent hours in worship in Jerusalem. Jewish leaders who knew about her would secretly come around to the back door so no one could see them, and they would ask for prayer and seek counsel.

Each year Sister Ruth would host a large holiday party at Halcyon House. Her team would decorate, cook, and bake for weeks in preparation. Regina attended her Christmas party one year and said, "The house was beautiful and many ministers, including the mayor, and many prominent leaders in Jerusalem, stopped by. Sister Ruth sang and played piano, and a sweet presence was there in the room. There was one Rabbi who came laying down in the back seat of a car and secretly entered through the back door."

Sister Ruth was highly regarded in Jerusalem and her home was a house of prayer for all nations and a sanctuary for those who wanted a touch from heaven. I will always remember the amazing work Sister Ruth did for the Lord in many nations. She went before kings and prominent leaders and was an influence to many nations for God.

ENCOUNTERS WITH GOD

Humble yourself before the Lord and pray. Live a life with prayer and turn from the things that offend God. If you want to experience the Glory, you must have a passionate heart and a hunger for God. Seek His face as Moses and David did with the right motivation to know Him intimately for who He is. God wants to reveal Himself to you as well as to know Him as a Person and have experiences and encounters with Him.

And this is eternal life, that they may know You, the only true God, and Jesus Christ whom you have sent. John 17:3 (NASB)

Be that eternal flame that never goes out and burns with passionate love for the Lord. Worship is a time of love. He wants to fellowship with you. He wants you to know Him intimately. If you seek Him with all your heart, you will find Him. He waits for you. He is preparing His Bride. Come, you are invited to enter His presence so He can show you more.

CHAPTER THREE

REV. RUTH HEFLIN VISITS THE PRAYER TOWER

John 4:23 (NASB) "But an hour is coming and now is, when the true worshipers will worship the Father in spirit and truth; for such people the Father seeks to be His worshipers."

In Manhattan, the Prayer Tower became recognized by ministers who traveled in and out of the NYC. Regina, Roberta, and I would coordinate the dinner parties for the Ministers and Missionaries who visited, and we would invite them to come and share a Bible study with our home fellowship group.

Sister Ruth would visit quite often at the Prayer Tower and spend time with our fellowship group. We would also have private meetings at Regina's home with Sister Ruth and she would pray for us and prophesy over us. It's so encouraging to hear from the Lord especially during times of trials and tribulations.

Regina, Roberta, and I were committed to praying for New York City, the Church, and the Nations, especially Israel. We were committed to praying for the Jewish people many of whom lived in New York. Over the twenty-five years of living in the city, I shared with many Jewish people, one on one, about Yeshua their Messiah who was slain for the sins of the world. He was the Lamb of God sacrificed on a tree and by His blood we are saved, forgiven, and redeemed.

I learned so much about the Glory of God through Sister Ruth's ministry. When she preached God's Word, she sang her message, and you could hear heaven echoing in her voice. She touched heaven as she sang, and glorified God and we ascended along with her in worship.

She taught us that a song releases the voice of the Spirit within us and builds us up. We also learned that as we praise the Lord in song that vision and revelation comes out of our mouths. She taught us that singing a new song does two things for you: it teaches you how to concentrate on God, and it teaches you simplicity. Ruth said, "Sing."

Use your voice to magnify the Lord. There is power in the Name of Jesus and when His Name is spoken out of your mouth, hell begins to lose its power. The Devil hates worship because it demolishes strongholds and demonic powers and principalities in the spirit realm.

We are to use our mouth to praise God or to sing to Him by telling him how much we love Him for all He has done. We were made for fellowship and intimacy with Him; that is why God created us.

God wants to bring enlargement in your life, and He brings it forth through your singing a new song to Him. Sing a new song that God has given you or sing a song that you know. One day as I was singing off key, the Holy Spirit reminded me that it doesn't matter if you can't hold a tune, by the time the sound gets to heaven it will be perfected. Therefore, sing until you get to the top of the hill. Be conscious that you are ascending the mountain of the Lord. Don't stop praising until you have entered in.

Through praising, we enter into His presence. Psalms 100:4 says, *"We enter His Gates with Thanksgiving and into His courts with Praise."* Praise is the entering in and the ascent upward. We must always be conscious of going up to the Holy Place -- continue praising until you get to the Holy Place.

"Who may ascend the hill of the Lord? Who may stand in his holy place? (Psalms 24:3, NIV).

Continual prayer and praise were one of the first things God taught the Jews. God instructed Moses in *Exodus 25:8, "Let them construct a sanctuary for Me, that I may Dwell among them."* He revealed how a special place was to be prepared for His Presence. *"Follow my pattern I give you, and my Presence will dwell with you."* God desires for His Presence and power to dwell among His People! The Tabernacle of Moses was designed according to God's pattern where the outer Court represented "Thanksgiving," the Holy Place represented "Praise," and the Holy of Holies represented "Worship." As you progressed, you were led to a place of deeper fellowship with the Lord and a greater manifestation of His glory! *Psalms 100:4 tells us to "Enter His gates with thanksgiving and His courts with praise."*

Moses aligned all the tribes physically around the four sides of the tabernacle, and they were aligned with each other in groups of three. As the twelve tribes of Israel were placed in order in groups of three around the Tabernacle, they were all facing the Ark that represented the presence of God and the Glory fire that was seen coming out of the Holy of Holies.

A place was created where God's Glory could dwell. As believers in Yeshua, that same Glory dwells in us. We are His dwelling place.

The church is to be a sanctuary of living stones where God is enthroned on the praises and worship of His people. It's where the supernatural power is to change the world. The Lord's presence is the only tangible substance to offer those who need a special touch from heaven!

ENCOUNTERS WITH GOD

Continual praise to the ancient Jews meant maintaining regular watches of prayer and praise each day. Be encouraged to get involved in your church and participate in prayer watches and praise as you prepare a sanctuary for His Presence. I encourage you to share your faith with your family members and those within your community. Let the glory within you flow forth so others can be set free. God desires His presence and power to dwell among His people. Do not settle for anything less than all that God has.

Let us pray. *Heavenly Father, in the Name of Jesus, I want more of you. You said that this is eternal life that I may know you. I want to know you more than yesterday. Set a fire down inside me that burns for you and your purposes. I commit myself to separating for your use so I can be a chosen vessel and carrier of your Glory***.**

CHAPTER FOUR

TOUCHING HEAVEN

Psalms 2:7,8 (NIV) "I will proclaim the decree of the Lord: He said to me, "You are My Son, today I have become your Father. Ask of Me, and I will make the Nations your inheritance, the ends of the earth your possession."

One evening during Sister Ruth's visit to New York City, we had a church meeting at the Prayer Tower. She sang her famous song, "I Ask for the Nations,"[a] and we all sang along with her and asked for the Nations and called them out by name.

As we worshiped, I felt like I was lifted to a higher dimension in the spirit. That's when I knew *I Touched Heaven* on behalf of the nations *and city*. Heaven invaded the service – the holy hush, the tangible presence of God was present – His Glory.

The Glory brought a knowing – you could feel Him-like a spiritual blanket covering over the entire room.

The Glory is an atmosphere that clothes you – you can't understand it with your mind – you have to enter into it. In the book of *Matthew 13:11(NASB), Jesus said, "To you it has been granted to know the mysteries of the kingdom of heaven..."*

That night, as our spirits ascended in praise, you could feel the Glory Presence as the spirit of worship came upon us. The Glory is His Presence. Praise brings the anointing to worship and worship brings the anointing of glory. In other words, you should praise until the worship comes, and worship until the glory falls.

Worship differs from praise. When you praise the Lord, *we will to praise*. But we *do not will to worship.* True worship happens when a believer's spirit is connected to God's Spirit and the spirit of worship comes upon you. Spiritual things become easy. If your mind is too involved with words, then you're too busy thinking and your spirit will not ascend. Oftentimes, if a congregation will sing a certain verse over and over again, the spirit of worship will come.

When we worship, we are focusing on the person of God; we find that there is an exchange of who we are for who He is. If we want to be changed, worship is the key. When we worship, we pour our hearts out to Him; we pour out our love for Him. He wants us to know Him as the Lover of our soul. God wants us to know Him; to feel His presence and worship Him in the beauty of holiness at His holy hill. His will is for us to seek to be worshipers above all else. *John 4:24 says, "God is spirit, and his worshipers must worship in spirit and in truth."*

God wants our praise and worship to bring us into the realm of revelation so we can be effective in prayer. For instance, as a prophetic intercessor, I rely on what God imprints in my spirit. The imprint in my spirit is like something being stamped in an instant. Therefore, your spirit needs to catch it instantly. Once it's caught, you pray by faith, and He fills you with His words as you speak forth what the Spirit of the Lord is saying. Therefore, when you pray over others, wait to see what the Spirit of revelation shows you so that you can have a sure word of encouragement for them.

It's all about God, not our gifts or talents, and what He wants to do in the earth and in people's lives. *Isaiah prophesies in chapter 46:10 (NIV): "I make known the end from the beginning, from ancient times, what is still to come. I say: My purpose will stand, and I will do all that I please."* We are His vessels and as we surrender to Him, He will do mighty things through us. God wants to manifest His Glory through us. We are His dwelling place. We're not here just to wait for Jesus to return.

One night, I was in my local church and there was such a heaviness in the meeting. The Pastor invited intercessors up to the front to pray because he sensed the heaviness. When I began to pray, I heard these words, "seek and destroy," then, the words coming out of my mouth were like a sniper in the realm of the spirit. It blew the oppression up and off the church service. It was like a fire coming forth out of my mouth - the heaviness left, and we continued on with the meeting. *"It's not by might, nor by power, but by my spirit says the Lord Almighty" (Zechariah 4:6, NIV).*

There is a difference between God's Anointing and God's Glory. *God's anointing* is what destroys the yokes and looses the bands of the enemy and wicked strongholds that are on yourself and others. *God's Glory* is His complete essence of who He is and His mighty power through supernatural encounters. When God's Glory shows up, it is tangible, and you feel a sense of heavy dignity.

The devil hates it when we pray and worship God because each time we do, the anointing destroys the works of the enemy, and the light of His Glory drowns out all darkness. Worship is the highest form of prayer.

If you are filled with the Spirit, speak forth what He shows you. The fire of the anointing inside you will accomplish the task in the spirit realm by the power of words coming forth from your mouth. The Lord will give you a knowing, a revelation of what's happening, or an imprint in the spirit, then He prays through you. *Prophetic authority means we say what God is saying*.

It's because of Heaven's influence that we know we are speaking what He has declared. All you need to do is open your mouth and pray it out. It's the voice of the Lord – The Lion of the Tribe of Judah. When He roars through you, everything stops. Be bold, be courageous, the Lord thy God is with you and working among you.

ENCOUNTERS WITH GOD

When you pray, ascend, with your mind and spirit, and touch Heaven as you ask for the Nations, and call them out by name. Nations are not just countries or groups of people, but they also include cultures, structural systems, and thought processes in various spheres of influence.

Let us pray. *Heavenly Father, show me my sphere of influence so I can show forth your Glory. Make me a house of prayer for the Nations.*

CHAPTER FIVE

CAMP MEETING

ENCOUNTERS IN HEAVENLY PLACES

2 Corinthians 3:18 (NASB) "But we all, with unveiled face, beholding as in a mirror the glory of the Lord, are being transformed into the same image from glory to glory, just as from the Lord, the Spirit."

It was the evening of July 2, 1985, and I was excited to be at the Campgrounds with Regina and Roberta and to see Sister Ruth. We were hungry to know more about the Lord. We looked forward to worshiping the King and to spending quality time seeking Him.

As you can imagine, life in NYC, the Big Apple, is hectic and everyone does everything in a New Yok minute. Sometimes it's so distracting that it's helpful to get out of town to have quality time with the Lord. So, every chance we could find during the summer months we would go to Camp meeting to rest and sit in the presence of the Lord.

At Calvary Campground, there was a very large outdoor sanctuary in the middle of the grounds where services were held throughout the day. No matter where you were on the campground, you could hear the praise music echoing throughout the grounds. The sound was very tranquil.

HEAVENLY ENCOUNTER ONE

Isaiah 6:1 (NIV) .... "I saw the Lord seated on a throne, high and exalted, and the train of his robe filled the temple."

It was evening at the Campground Sanctuary, and you could feel the strong presence of the Lord. As we were worshipping the Lord, I saw two "feathered wings" (Psalms 91:4) clapping together behind the pulpit. Then as I raised my head upward to worship, I saw a vision of large scrolls opening and closing, opening and closing. It was compared to a curtain opening and closing except they were scrolls. The Spirit was getting my attention because I wasn't sure what I was seeing. When the Lord is trying to get your attention, most times there is a repetition. When I finally submitted to what I was seeing, the scrolls rolled back, and heaven opened before me. I saw an orchestra of singers, the heavenly choir praising and singing the same song we were singing on earth. As my eyes traveled up their arms to the top of their hands that were lifted high, I saw Jesus, high and lifted up. He had on a translucent blue robe; and, staring at the stillness of His body, spoke an overwhelming peace to me. He was amazingly beautiful–a picture that no one could ever paint or capture. Every feature of His being ministered and demonstrated the character of who He is. In looking at His cheeks I saw mercy, and in his eyes, I saw compassion. The beauty of His stillness was beyond peace. My eyes were like a telescopic lens that only captured what Jesus wanted me to see. Every aspect of His being tells a story of His divine Nature and Character. All His features mirror traits of His divine nature in an ineffable and eternal majesty. Every expression of love is found in His countenance of most holy beauty. When you see the beauty of the Lord it holds your whole heart captive and stays with you forever. His beauty is beyond anything you would ever see or compare it to. His countenance of eternal beauty is filled with a wondrous splendor. Seeing the Lord face to face changes you forever and there is still more to come.

God wants you to look at Him face to face. He wants you to see His eyes, His checks. He wants you to know Him in ways you have not known Him. He created us for intimacy and fellowship with Him. Nothing you desire should compare with your love for the Lord. It's an all-consuming fire with love for the Lord, to know Him more and more. Live only to love Him.

After this heavenly encounter, I could not tell anyone what I saw – I was absolutely speechless. All I could do was write it in my journal. It has taken all these years for the Lord to release me to share it with you in this book. More and more believers are experiencing encounters of seeing Jesus face-to-face and the beauty of His Holiness.

HEAVENLY ENCOUNTER TWO

John 10:9 (NASB) "I am the door; if anyone enters through Me, he will be saved, and will go in and out and find pasture."

The next morning at the Campgrounds, I could hear the music coming from the Sanctuary. This morning Sister Ruth was ministering, and my spirit was excited to receive what she had to say. I made my way to the Sanctuary, and in the front of the altar, we are praising and worshiping the King of Glory.

As I was standing at the altar, I began to feel a weight on me that got heavier and heavier as I stood up. It's as though I wanted to lie down. I heard the Spirit say, "It's okay just lie down, trust me." Since I couldn't stand any longer anyway because of the weight of the glory, I did lie down before the altar. While on the floor, my spirit was lifted, and I saw myself walking on a cobble stone path barefooted. Angels were on either side in a row along the path rejoicing with joy as I walked. Looking ahead as I walked, I saw Jesus standing at this very tall brown wooden door with a staff in His hand waiting for me. Looking from afar, Jesus wore a natural burlap-like shepherd's garment. When I reached Him, He opened the door fully and invited me in. He and I walked and traveled over many, many green pastures, over hills, through vivid green pastures in many different sizes. The greenery was vividly bright because of the Glory of heaven. The flowers in Heaven were mind altering colors like you have never seen. They were alive as though they could speak as they moved in heaven's atmosphere. Through this heavenly encounter, Jesus taught me that He was the Chief Shepherd, and that heaven is a real place (*2 Corinthians 12:2, NASB*).

What does a good shepherd do? The good shepherd lays down his life for the sheep. The role of a shepherd is to lead his sheep to green pastures, to protect them from predators, to make sure that none get lost or go astray. A shepherd is a symbol of protection, power, and authority. That's who our Jesus is, the Good Shepherd!

At the Camp Meetings, Sister Ruth always wanted to know what the people were hearing when the Glory came. This time, I openly shared this encounter that the Lord had given me and everyone in the service started to rejoice. What a morning. What an evening – I will never forget the countenance of the eternal beauty of the Lord.

As a young believer in Christ, I would press the Lord in prayer about seeing His Glory. It was part of my prayer time with Him. You can do the same. Seek Him and you will find Him. He is no respecter of persons – ask of Him and he will give you the desires of your heart. It's the busyness of life that keeps you from seeking Him. It's good to get away from the hustle and bustle of life in order to seek the Lord. Remember, we have an enemy that does not want you to grow in prayer and worship. The enemy wants to keep you busy and carnal. Say no to busyness and shift your attention.

When you move in the Glory realm, things start to happen. The Glory brings a smoothness, like gliding or like an eagle flying with its wings spread out as the wind carries him effortlessly. In that tangible place of His Glory there is absolutely nothing to say because you are filled with God Himself. We were designed to fit seamlessly in the Glory. Every believer is wired to recognize Him and respond to Him as we walk in obedience.

In the Glory, we are impacted so we can impact everything around us. In the Glory, something shifts about our perspective. There are so many dimensions of His presence and there is still more. It's in the richness of His grace He made us alive together with Christ. *He raised us up with Him and seated us with Him in the heavenly places in Christ Jesus, so that in the ages to come (it's continuous) He might show the surpassing riches of His grace in kindness toward us in Christ Jesus (Ephesians 2:6, NASB).*

In 2 Chronicles 5:13, when they sang as one, the glory-cloud came. Likewise, God filled the Tabernacle of Moses and Solomon's Temple. How much more will He fill us, His Temple. God's goal is to fill the whole earth with His Glory. *Psalms 72:19 (NASB)...And may the whole earth be filled with His glory. Amen and Amen.*

We were born for this seamless interaction between us and the King of Glory. People who dwell in His presence will carry His presence and by doing so, will bring change.

Every Spirit-filled believer has the privilege of bringing the glory into their churches, home, and community. We do it through our voices. The lifting up of the voice brings about a different atmosphere. You want the deep calling too deep to flow out of you for others.

If we're going to see an increase of the glory on the earth, it will be through you, *"Christ in you, the Hope of Glory, Colossians 1:27."* We must become familiar with the Glory and the message He is wanting to convey.

HEAVENLY ENCOUNTER THREE

John 11:40 (NASB) "Did I not say to you that if you believe, you will see the glory of God?"

The following morning, it was my last day at the Campgrounds before heading back to Manhattan. The Lord had filled me with so much of Himself. My spirit was overflowing with the love and goodness of the Lord, and I couldn't wait to get to the morning service.

Sister Ruth's brother, Rev. Wallace, was preaching in the morning service. During the worship, I was standing at the altar, and I felt like my spirit was ascending and found myself walking down a cement pathway and I saw in front of me a white mansion. As I approached the mansion, I saw a very tall front entrance door that was opened by a slim crack. Next to the entrance door on either side were very large cement flowerpots with torching flames of fire coming out of the center of the pots. As I approached the door, I managed to squeeze myself through the crack of the door to go inside. Inside was dark, but against the wall was a huge angel with wings that stood from the bottom of his feet over to the top of his head. He was standing guard. He would not look at me or give any type of acknowledgement. Not sure what to do next, I remember asking Jesus to show me what was in the room. Then suddenly, I saw glimpses of eyes and legs that flashed before me. I understood what the Lord wanted me to glean, and I wept so hard. Can you image that God has a room inside a heavenly mansion that houses body parts such as eyes and legs? What a good God we serve!

After the service, I shared openly what I saw, and people at the camp lined up behind me for healing. I laid hands on everyone who came forth and they were all touched by the Lord. What a supernatural morning; God showed up!

Can you just see how good our God is, full of love and compassion for His people that there are rooms in heaven housing body parts? The Lord can do whatever He purposes to do. He's the Lord God Almighty over our life. He can give you new eyes -- He can give you new legs. He is Lord, the King of the Universe, and we are His. We were created to be loved by the King. We are His, the Bride of Christ.

Nothing is impossible to them that believe. Things become easier when we just believe what the Lord says in His Word. Say His Words out loud, hear yourself say it, use your mouth to speak into existence what He is saying to you.

ENCOUNTERS WITH GOD

It's time to arise and take your place seated with the King in heavenly places (Ephesians 2:6). It's time to create with the words of your mouth what you would like to see as opposed to what you see in your life. If you turn your negative confession around, you will see results in your personal life. Meditate on the scriptures that best tell you how God sees your situation and speak it forth.

At the time of writing this book, we are living in the Hebraic decade of 5780. The Hebraic letter that symbolizes the decade of *5780* is the letter Pey. The letter Pey actually means 'mouth' in Hebrew. In this decade, we are to use our mouth to praise and make declarations from the Scriptures for God's purposes.

The Bride of Christ is to speak forth the Bridegroom's words. We are to Roar like the Lion of Judah (Jesus/ Yeshua), and decree and declare His Glory. Your voice is a weapon in the realm of the spirit and the devil hates it, and he will do whatever he can to muzzle it. Let's not be unaware of his wicked schemes.

The power to change is in your mouth. The power for health, healing, prosperity, or whatever you need, are in your mouth! It says in Job, 22:28 (NASB) "You will also decree a thing, and it will be established for you; And light will shine on your ways."

CHAPTER SIX

YESHUA IN THE BIG APPLE

Ephesians 3:6 (NIV) "This mystery is that through the gospel the Gentiles are heirs together with Israel, members together of one body, and sharers together in the promise of Christ Jesus."

It was time to leave the Campgrounds and head back to Manhattan. I met so many wonderful people at the Camp. One person, in particular, that I wanted to meet was the Psalmist Worship Leader at the services. Her name was Rev. Gwendolyn Sims Warren. Sister Gwen was an amazing Psalmist Worship Leader. With just a few touches on the keyboard, the Glory would fall immediately. You had to be there to catch it. It was the anointing on her life in music and the Glory of His presence on her life through praise and worship that made her extraordinary in the Lord. I so much wanted to meet her personally before leaving the camp but did not get the opportunity to do so at that time.

Back in New York City, my husband Bruce picked me up from the airport. He was a dashing young man full of wit and humor. He was a Jewish believer and young in the Lord. We were married for one year, but it didn't go without a lot of conflicts. We were both young and had a lot of issues the first year of marriage that were so difficult to resolve.

He was on fire for the Lord. In his spare time, he drove a taxicab around the city and shared his faith with the passengers into the late hours since New York never slept. Bruce studied the scriptures and was flowing in amazing revelations of his Jewish Messiah, Yeshua Hamashiach. As an evangelist, he was so on fire for the Lord, he shared the good news about the Messiah wherever he went.

In the city, we also attended *Jews for Jesus* and gleaned a lot about our Jewish Messiah and the Hebraic roots of Christianity. We learned that it was God's plan to make Gentiles Fellow Heirs together with Jesus, enabling them to experience all of the blessings of Israel's Messiah. This was the mystery as described in Ephesians Chapter 3 that had been hidden since the foundation of the world. God's plan was, through the church, to graft believing Gentiles into His covenant so they also could receive His blessings.

Ephesians 2:11-19 describes it this way:

"Remember that you Gentiles were separate from Messiah, excluded from citizenship in Israel and foreigners to the covenants of the promise, without hope and without God in the world..." "But now in Messiah Jesus you (Gentiles) who were far away have been brought near..."

"His purpose was to create ONE NEW MAN out of the two (Jews and Gentiles). Consequently, you (believing Gentiles) are no longer foreigners and aliens, but fellow citizens with God's people (believing Jews) and members of God's household!"[2]

The church is God's way of including the Gentiles in the blessings of Israel's covenant. Every good thing that you receive from God is a result of being grafted into the Hebraic roots of Christianity. The scriptures say, *"Salvation is from the Jews."* (John 4:22) Through the Jews we have received the Scriptures, the covenants, and His promises. The Church draws its life from their Jewish roots.

As we read the book of Romans, we learn that from the Jews we received the Bible, the promises of God and the covenants. From the Jews, we have the revelation of God's character as well as godly examples from men like Abraham, Moses, and David. And from the Jews we have Yeshua Hamashiach, Jesus the Messiah.

Ephesians 2:21-22 (NASB) tells us that the ultimate goal of the One New Man is revival! The Apostle Paul says when Jew and Gentile are fitted together, they form a holy temple in the Lord, a dwelling in which God lives by his Spirit!

We have not yet seen the church restored to its Jewish roots, but we are living in the days of restoration. Acts 3:21 promises that before Jesus returns, God will bring restoration in the earth. God is calling the church back to its roots and to become the One New Man where Jews and

Gentiles will feast together on God's new covenant. God is coming back for His glorious Church. He is preparing His Bride and bringing restoration to the Church. It's time for the church to rise up in power and demonstration and glory. His Kingdom has come!

BOROUGH PARK HOME OF THE HASIDIC

John 4:22 (NASB) "...for salvation is from the Jews."

Most weekends, Bruce and I would spend time with his mom and dad. We would share our faith in the Messiah with them. They lived in Borough Park, Brooklyn where most of the Hasidic Jews lived.

Hasidic Judaism is a Jewish religious group that arose as a spiritual revival movement in the territory of contemporary Western Ukraine during the 18th Century and spread rapidly throughout Eastern Europe. Borough Park is home to many Hasidic groups. Many prayers were declared on the streets of Borough Park that the eyes of their understanding would be enlightened and that the veil would be removed from their eyes so they could see the truth that Yeshua Hamashiach is their Jewish Messiah.

You will read about Yeshua in the Old Testament from Isaiah the Prophet's writings starting in Chapter 52 verse 13. This is perhaps the strongest of the Messianic prophecies. It describes the priestly ministry of the Messiah, who would die as an innocent offering for the sins of the Jewish people.

The prophecy has numerous points of fulfillment recorded in the Gospel accounts of the death of the Messiah.[3] He was "like a lamb led to the slaughter," an innocent sufferer who died on behalf of others. God's heart is that all Israel will be saved (Romans 9:26). The Jewish people's acceptance of Yeshua as their Messiah will lead to worldwide revival. In *Romans 11:15 (TPT),* we read, *"For if their temporary rejection released the reconciling power of grace into the world, what will happen when Israel is reinstated and reconciled to God? It will unleash resurrection power throughout the whole earth!"*

I am grateful to the Lord that within a short time, both of my in-laws gave their heart to Yeshua, their Messiah. Elsie Wasserman, my mother-in-law, was a picture of gentleness and love. I look forward to seeing both in-laws again in heaven as we celebrate and glorify God together.

Each one of us is searching for something to fill the void we feel in our heart. Each of us is searching for truth and the purpose of life. Only Yeshua, Jesus can fill the void and give purpose. God designed it that way so we can find our way back to Him. The material things of this world only fill us temporarily. But, when you find Yeshua, that void you feel is filled with overflowing rivers of life.

If you would like to know Yeshua as your Messiah, then speak to God in this prayer:

> *Abba Father, I believe that You are the One mankind has been searching for and that the only way to connect with You is through Yeshua (Jesus) the Messiah of the Jewish people. I ask You to come into my heart and reveal Yourself to me by your Spirit and truth. I believe that Yeshua is the way and the truth, therefore I choose to follow You. Amen.*

ENCOUNTERS WITH GOD

Praying for Israel is a key to world revival.

- Take a stand and pray for God's purposes to be fulfilled in Israel and all the Jewish people.
- Pray that the Jewish people will be awakened and behold their Messiah, Yeshua Hamashiach, who died for the sins of the world.
- Cry out to God that *"all Israel will be saved."* (Romans 11:26, NASB)
- Go before the Lord today and pray that God's Glory will cover the earth as the waters cover the sea, to bring an awakening, a worldwide revival and transformation!
- Also, pray that the Spirt of Truth and Justice will prevail in your nation and your city.
  "When the righteous increase, the people rejoice." (Proverbs 29:2, NASB)

Let us pray: Abba Father, in Yeshua's Name, we lift up the nation of Israel and the Jewish people. You Lord are their strength and stronghold in times of trouble. We thank you that Israel is under your protection and divine guidance. Your Word says that, *"all Israel shall be saved!"* **We pray for** *"the peace of Jerusalem. May they prosper that love you. May peace be within your walls and prosperity within your palaces."* **(Psalms 122: 6,7, NASB).**

CHAPTER SEVEN

REV. GWENDOLIN WARREN

THE CRUCIFIED LIFE

Psalms 150:6 "Let everything that hath breath, praise the Lord."

A few months had gone by from when I last visited the Camp. Surprisingly, I just heard from a fellow believer that Sister Gwen, the Psalmist Worship Leader at the camp, moved to Brooklyn. I was thrilled when I heard it and started to find out exactly where she was.

One day, moved by God's Spirit, I boldly took the train out to Felix Street in Brooklyn and knocked on her front door. When she answered I introduced myself and told her I saw her at the Camp as she ministered in music and that I knew Sister Ruth. She invited me in.

I shared with her that the purpose of my visit was to let her know that the believers in the city needed her.

Manhattan was dry and the believers needed to be taught to understand the Glory. I cried when I told her how much she was needed. She thanked me for visiting and said she would pray. Well, soon afterwards she started a home group, and I was her first member. Her fellowship, Breath of Life Ministries, grew so much in a short period of time we had to relocate.

Thanks to my friend Regina, Sister Gwen relocated to the Empire State Building on the 68th floor. Thereafter, for twenty years, Sister Gwen was my Pastor and Mentor in New York City. Sitting under her leadership, we lived in the Glory realm every time the prayer warriors got together for prayer, praise, and fellowship. The glory and anointing on her life as Pastor, Worship Psalmist, and Teacher was incomparable. Each time the fellowship met, she taught God's Word and there was always a strong move of the Spirit because she carried the Glory.

To introduce a little of her background, Sister Gwendolin Sims Warren studied music and opera in Austria and Oberlin Conservatory of Music in Ohio. She performed at Lincoln Center, with the Metropolitan Opera and the Boston Symphony, and throughout Europe. She was a recipient of the coveted Marian Anderson Award and Lilli Lehman Bronze Medal for Excellence from the International Mozarteum Foundation, Salzburg. She was an amazing woman of God as she led the Body of Christ to an in-depth understanding of Praise and Worship through scriptural study and demonstration.

Sister Gwen must have taught 1,000 messages on dying

to self. In John 12:24 (NASB) says, *"Truly, truly I say to you, unless a grain of wheat falls into the earth and dies, it remains alone; but if it dies, it bears much fruit."*

She would teach us, "When you get up to minister at the pulpit, people need to see the spirit of Jesus and not flesh." We always had to be prayed-up in prayer before each church service to bring our flesh under so we could be sensitive to the Holy Spirit and effective in the lives of others. She understood the glory realm and she did not want flesh activated. She wanted unity so the glory of God could manifest. Sister Gwen had a thorough understanding of the Glory and the Holiness of God. That is why when we met for services, the presence of the Lord was so strong. In fact, the Shekinah Gory of God (Shekinah means "to dwell") usually manifested in our midst when we got together to pray. During church services, everything was built around the moving of the Holy Spirit. The Holy Spirit was the priority. It was all about hosting the presence of God.

Much of the Old Testament was written to teach the Hebrew people how to experience His presence on a continual basis. She set an example of what a church should be. Many times, Sister Gwen would just play chords and sing in the spirit and a prophetic flow would bring heaven down. There was a sound that you could hear on her voice that echoed from the heavens. You could hear the overtones of heaven when she worshiped at the piano. We all grew spiritually because we soaked in the Glory and lived a life of prayer. We understood and worked at living the crucified life.

The Apostle Paul writes in Galatians 2:20 (NASB) "I have been crucified with Christ; and it is no longer I who live, but Christ lives in me; and the life which I now live in the flesh I live by faith in the Son of God, who loved me and gave Himself up for me."

Never reject an opportunity to die to self. Our job is to surrender to the cross – His job is resurrection. For example, don't let envy or jealousy overtake your life. When you feel those pangs within, you have an opportunity for the cross. Rejecting the opportunity to die to self, is to reject the resurrection and reward. Did you know that God appoints certain times in your life to die to self?

> *The Prophet Hosea writes in Chapter 2:14,15, 20, ".... I will lead her (Israel) into the desert and speak tenderly to her there. I will return her vineyards to her and transform the Valley of Trouble (Valley of Achor), into a gateway of hope. She will give herself to me there, as she did long ago when she was young,.....I will be faithful to you and make you mine, and you will finally know me as the Lord" (NLT).*

In the crucified life, God leads us into the desert and cleans us up; then, shows us His never-ending compassion, faithfulness, and unfailing love. His tenderness and goodness draws us back to Him.

ENCOUNTERS WITH GOD

Today, pray and memorize this scripture - *"I have been crucified with Christ; and it is no longer I who live, but Christ lives in me; and the life which I now live in the flesh I live by faith in the Son of God, who loved me and gave Himself up for me."*

Let us pray: *Heavenly Father, in Jesus Name, help me to live a life worthy of you. I want to live in your presence because in your presence, is fullness of joy. Show me the way in which I am to go and help me to fulfill my purpose of what is written in my book in heaven. I want to fulfill every page of destiny written about me.*

Now believe that He has heard you and stand on His promises.

CHAPTER EIGHT

BURNING ONES

Colossians 1:27(NIV) "To them God has chosen to make known among the Gentiles the glorious riches of this mystery, which is Christ in you the hope of glory."

We must become familiar with the glory realm like never before. I've visited church services where the Minister did not know what to do in the "holy hush" manifested Glory. Most Ministers could not even get to that point due to all the many interruptions in the service with announcements, etc. All that which is not related to worship creates a spiritual whiplash -- an atmosphere of being in and out of the spirit. Worship has a protocol as seen in the Old Testament Tabernacle. It was built according to God's pattern: first the outer Court, The Holy Place, then the Holy of Holies. We are to "*Enter his gates with thanksgiving and his courts with praise...*" *(Psalms 100:4)*. It is a journey from flesh to Spirit.

In the realm of worship and glory, it's the one thing that fully satisfies why we're alive – His manifested presence. We were born and designed to live in the Glory of God. We become arrested and our heart burns with affection for Him, it's the burning place of deep affection for who He is. We were born to be partners with Almighty God and to dwell in His glory!

Our God is the eternal flame. We are to go after more of God. Don't let God's fire that dwells in you to go out or become lukewarm. Becoming lukewarm is where your flesh is comfortable.

In *Leviticus 9:23-24 (NASB), Moses and Aaron went into the tent of meeting. When they came out and blessed the people, the glory of the Lord appeared to all the people. Then fire came out from before the Lord and consumed the burnt offering and the portions of fat on the altar; and when all the people saw it, they shouted and fell on their faces.*

It's time for the remnant to call fire down from heaven– to change our lifestyle from lukewarm to a passionate burning one. Those who are lukewarm need revival. Never let the fire burn out or reject God's fullness. God is gathering His remnant in this hour. When the fire touches you, it marks you forever. Keep the fire burning – a perpetual eternal flame that must never go out.

I remember one summer evening Sister Gwen had a ministry meeting in a church located in Harlem. It was a spectacular time in the Lord. Apostle Joel Laurore was Sister Gwen's apostolic covering, and he was visiting at the time to minister at the church. Apostle Joel has a ministry in Tulsa, OK called World Revival Temple. He had many Missionaries under his covering stationed all over the world. Apostle Joel, even to this day, is saturated with the presence of God. You can hear the echo of heaven on his voice when he speaks. God's presence is so strong, that your body actually quivers when he preaches. When he and Sister Gwen ministered together, it was incredibly powerful and with such ease. Under this ministry, your life changed from faith to faith and glory to glory. This is what church is supposed to be about.

At the Harlem service, Sister Gwen was ministering at the piano in worship when I saw this scroll like smoke coming out from both sides of the wall, at the center of the altar. It was billowing out slowly to the floor. As the people were dancing in the isles, this smoke like substance rose up to the waists of the people. You could not see the people from the waist down as they were dancing because the smoke of God's glory covered them. The Glory of the Lord was visiting us. The time came when God's Glory rolled up like a scroll and left the same way it came. Sister Gwen continued to worship while playing the piano and there was such a thick presence of heaven. This was the Glory Realm. When you are in this type of atmosphere, you change, you get healed, you get revelation, you no longer have to strive.

There are times that the Glory will come down as spiritual drops of rain. Other times, it may come as a spiritual mist. Some people see the glory as sparkles. I have personally experienced all these types of glory manifestations.

I had a friend who recently called me and said her teenage son, a creative artist and musician, was praising in his room and when he came out to the living room, gold sparkles were all over his face and hands. She took a picture of her son and sent me a text message so I could see it for myself. Some of the most beautiful expressions of love have come from young believers. Their love for the Lord is fresh. Jesus said, *"have you never read, 'From the lips of children and infants you have ordained praise?'" (Matthew 21:16, NIV).*

Through a lifestyle of worship, the Lord wants to take us up in vision to His Throne. He wants you to look upon His face. He wants you to see His eyes. He wants you to see His cheeks. He wants you to know Him intimately so that you can present Him to others and can describe Him from personal experience, from having seen Him, from having heard His voice, from having felt His touch. *Jesus said, "This is eternal life that they may know you, the only true God, and Jesus Christ whom you have sent" (John 17:3, NASB).* We are only beginning to see the glorious day of the Lord.

God's Word says He is coming back for a glorious church, *"that He might present to Himself the church in all her glory, having no spot or wrinkle or any such thing; but that she would be holy and blameless (Ephesians 5:27, NASB).* But when you look at the church you may say, "How is that going to happen?" Well, the Lord knows just how to maneuver His Ekklesia (His called-out ones), His remnant, to get them to that place in Him.

Jesus said, ...and on this rock I will build my church (Ekklesia) and the gates of Hades will not overpower it (Mark 16:18).

The Ekklesia, (His called-out ones) His remnant, are those believers who choose to pull away from the larger group of church goers and are separate unto God. As the Ekklesia of God, we are the governmental body of the cosmos. The Ekklesia is God's legislative governing body on earth, not just the Bride of Christ. We are called to sit on thrones to influence creation. You execute your power of influence by allowing Christ, who is in you, to be revealed through you. Every Spirit-filled believer has the privilege of bringing the Glory into their churches and home.

"To whom God willed to make known what is the riches of the glory of this mystery among the Gentiles, which is Christ in you, the hope of glory" (Colossians 1:27, NASB).

The Glory of the Lord is within you. Wherever you go, you carry the glory. When you speak, the glory is in your voice. It is time to let the "hope of glory" come out and be a blessing to others wherever you go. To be a burning glory carrier, spend intimate time with the Lord in prayer and praise and worship. Let God have His way with you – surrender your all to Him and He won't disappoint you.

ENCOUNTERS WITH GOD

In Luke 3:16 (TPT), John the Baptizer made it clear by telling them, "There is one coming who is mightier than I. .... I can only baptize you in this river, but he will baptize you into the Spirit of holiness and into his raging fire."

Fire is the outward sign and recognizable indication that something inside you changed. Without the fire, flesh is on the throne and not God.

Revivalists burn with fire for more of God and His purposes. Never let your fire burn out or reject God's fullness.

In the Name of Jesus, I release the fire of the presence of God to those who hunger for it. I pray for the fire to purify and sanctify your life and for a passion for saving souls. Once you are ignited with the fire of God, go and be a witness for Jesus. Call the lost to salvation, heal the sick, and deliver the captives. God will give you the supernatural boldness as you go forward preaching and teaching and confirming the Gospel of Jesus Christ with signs, wonders, and miracles. I release the Glory of God over your life and your family!

CHAPTER NINE

TIMES SQUARE HERE WE COME

Habakkuk 2:14 (NIV) "For the earth will be filled with the knowledge of the glory of the Lord, as the waters cover the sea."

After a few years praying for the Nations and the City, the Prayer Tower was beginning to get more recognition by visiting Pastors and many Ministry Leaders. Ministers who arrived in NYC, all had an open invitation to come to the Tower to pray.

One day, Sister Gwen received a call from Pastor David Wilkerson. David Wilkerson moved to New York City to start up a church right in the heart of Times Square called the Times Square Church.

He grew up in Pennsylvania. His father and grandfather were pastors. David, a country preacher, would visit NYC to minister in the ghettos with drug addicts and delinquents. As a result of his visits, Teen Challenge was birthed. It is a world-wide Christian organization for drug addicts, delinquents, and other troubled youths. His book, *The Cross and the Switchblade* was a result of his labor for the Lord. Pastor David was a well-known speaker and respected authority on the floundering younger generation.

As Pastor David was settling in the city, he heard about Sister Gwen's "Breath of Life Ministries" at the Empire State Building and began inquiring about us. Pastor David's inquiries ultimately led to a merger between the two churches. He offered Sister Gwen a new opportunity to lead the music ministry and choir at Times Square Church. What a wonderful opportunity that opened for her – it was a perfect fit in every way and was her time of convergence. So, we all merged to Times Square Church and thrived under this ministry.

Our small church grew overnight to one thousand people and then quickly expanded in growth. The only place Pastor David could find to house all the people was a theatre. Therefore, in due time, we moved to the Mark Hellinger Theatre on 51st Street and Broadway and this ministry is still thriving as of today.

Pastor David was a true prophet and teacher. His messages on sin were riveting. Between Pastor David's messages on sin and Pastor Gwen's messages on dying to self, you had no other choice but to get your life together quickly. Although they both had a zero tolerance for sin and fleshly deeds, they were full of love and compassion. You had to be a tough Christian in NYC because sin was all around you as you walked around Manhattan. It's only when you face your sin and give it to the Lord that you will be set free from your fears and anxiety.

Sister Gwen thrived in all she touched. She was an outstanding woman of God in life and character. She loved and made room for everyone that needed a touch from heaven. Throughout the years I was with her, I saw her abound and I saw her abased as she followed Christ with a whole heart. Because of the glory on her life, she struggled with much opposition. It was the prayers of intercession that brought her through the trials.

ENCOUNTERS WITH GOD

Whether you're on a city street or wherever you go, there is someone to reach with God's glory. Now, the harvest is ripe and ready. Most times as you're walking, you will find the people just sitting and waiting – they are waiting for you. That's when God's divine appointment shows up and you are able to share the gospel of salvation.

In Mark 16:20, then the disciples went out and preached everywhere, and the Lord worked with them and confirmed his world by the signs that accompanied it.

The Lord will work with you. We struggle with spiritual things but it's the spiritual that breaks through the natural. As believers, we learn that the Holy Spirit pulls us out of the natural into the spirit to access God and have the God kind of life.

When you are born again of the spirit, you enter into a spiritual dimension in God. A whole other realm is open to you. Being born again (receiving Jesus Christ as your Lord and Savior) gives you spiritual manifestations of God for you to lean into and catch. You are to believe and obey His Word and see the amazing things He will do in your life. As believers, it's time that we manifest His Glory in the earth. The moment you believe, *IT SHALL BE SO!*

The world is waiting for you to release the glory that lives within you. Jesus said to His disciples, *"Go into all the world and preach the gospel to every creature."*

(Mark 16:15, NASB). In this hour, the harvest is so ripe and waiting for you to reach out and share all that Christ has done. I challenge you to make the decision to go into your world (home, business, city) and testify of Jesus. This is the time for the manifestation of the glory in and through believers. The demonstration of the supernatural follow those who go and obey.

Let us pray: *Lord, have your way with me. I repent of my sin and ask that you wash and cleanse me of all my unrighteousness. I pray that you revive the ministerial and motivational gifts you put inside me. I want to be ignited by the fire of the presence of God and a passion for saving souls. Not my way but your way in my life*.

CHAPTER TEN

THE GOD OF ALL COMFORT

Mark 10:8 (NIV) "And the Two Shall Become One Flesh; so they are no longer two, but one flesh."

My husband Bruce and I served together with Sister Gwen until we merged to Times Square Church. Sadly enough, Bruce backslid into his old lifestyle.

We had a hard time in our marriage the first two years and all the issues seemed to have escalated. A friend called me one evening and said Bruce was going to clubs after work. I also found out later that he was being unfaithful to the marriage. I was devastated by the news because it was contrary to what we believed.

Remembering God's Word that He hated divorce, I did not give up; and took Bruce back even after his unfaithfulness. Confronting the issues, we decided to go for marital counseling. I quickly set-up a meeting with one of the Pastors at Times Square Church for marriage counseling. Bruce agreed to go, and I was focused on getting our marriage healed and back on the right track.

It was an early winter morning, with fresh snow on the ground, I arrived at the Times Square Church Pastor's office for my meeting and waited for Bruce to arrive. When Bruce arrived a few minutes later, he opened the office door and entered, but started to speak while still standing at the door. He said, "I know you think I'm here for counseling but I'm here to tell you I'm leaving." With that he turned around and walked out the door. I was speechless, I was frozen inside and felt very ashamed. It was like a sword had pierced my soul. All I could do was thank the Pastor for his time and I left the office.

On the street and walking home in the cold weather, I was devastated. Torn inside, it was as though the walls of my spirit had fallen. I prayed, "Lord help me." I could not get it together. Sometimes, your prayers to the Father in times of need, are one or two words, or sometimes just a sigh. He knows what is happening in your life and He's there for you.

I felt ashamed to tell Sister Gwen about the breakup since we both served as leaders in the ministry. When a marriage breaks up, it's like pulling the flesh off your bones because a marriage is a Covenant before God that makes a man and a woman "one flesh." This is why God hates divorce. The whole experience was excruciatingly painful to live through. I had to work through the loneliness, the shame, the feeling of being disgraced and abandoned and the big "R" word - Rejection. I did not like my story – it was too hard.

For the next few years, all I could do was go to work and then go home and put my praise and worship music on. I repented of everything I could think of. I searched my soul and asked the Lord to deliver me from all unrighteousness, such as pride, religion, and self-righteousness. I forgave everyone who may have hurt me.

I did not want to get stuck in this bad story. I allowed the Holy Spirit to re-parent me. The Holy Spirit became my mother, my father, my everything. The Holy Spirit whom Jesus sent to the disciples after He was resurrected became my Comforter! I learned to rely on Him!

We are to forgive and move forward with our eyes lifted up to the Lord. I forgave myself and my husband and my soul was set free from being held captive as I continued in the healing process. *Psalms 34:5 (NIV) says, "those who look to Him are radiant; their faces are never covered with shame."* During this time of healing most of my prayers were "God protect me" because it felt like the walls of my spirit were broken down.

You have to lean on the arm of Christ to bring you through the process of healing. One cannot rebuke pain and tell it to go. You have to daily work out the process through prayer and meditating on God's Word.

One night I cried in my bed with sobbing tears. Suddenly, I could feel a wind enter the bedroom and a strong presence of the Lord. It arrested me. I could feel

Him sweep into my room. Jesus bent over next to me and I could feel Him stroke my head and long brown hair. I felt so much peace permeate my room; I felt so much love and comfort beyond words. What a God we serve! His love will never fail us. If you believe in Him, He will show up in your darkest moments. He will never leave you or forsake you.

Thank God for Sister Gwen who prayed me through this crisis. She never gave up on me and remained a true Pastor and friend for twenty-five years thereafter.

I allowed God to heal my wounds so that I could break free from shame. We don't need to hide behind shame because the window of grace is open to escape through the Cross of Jesus. *Hebrews 12:2 (NIV) says, "Let us fix our eyes on Jesus, the author and perfecter of our faith, who for the joy set before him endured the cross, scorning its shame, and sat down at the right hand of the throne of God."* The cross is a symbol of victory and not a symbol of shame.

In defeating the lies of the enemy, the devil will try to take what's wrong and make us believe it's who we are. If you believe the lies, you will label yourself with a stamp of self-condemnation. Our past failures are not who we are. Just because we fail is not an indication that we are failures. If you believe these lies of the enemy, it will cause limitations and stagnation.

As a believer in Christ, you are set free from all condemnation of the past. Through the shed blood of Jesus Christ on the cross, we are redeemed, justified and reconciled and can do all things through Christ who strengthens us.

I love this verse in Psalms 139:16 (NIV), *"your eyes saw my unformed body. All the days ordained for me were written in your book before one of them came to be."* You have been qualified by God to do all He has called you to do. The devil will try to stop every spirit filled believer from walking in power and purpose.

Psalms 40:2 (NASB) says, *"He brought me up out of the pit of destruction, out of the miry clay, And he set my feet upon a rock making my footsteps firm."*

Believe the good news of the gospel. He knows you by name and has a plan for your life, one of hope and a future.

The good news is that Jesus is married to the backslider. After several years, Bruce did rededicate his life back to Yeshua which was an answer to many prayers.

ENCOUNTERS WITH GOD

I would like to caution you. If you're young in the Lord, I would counsel you to wait and not rush into marriage. Make sure your motives are right, so you don't get married for the wrong reasons. Take time to know each other. Take time to know the Lord and pray until you get an answer. You can never out wait God.

There are many people who dive into the shallow end of love. For example, loneliness, sexual frustration, some sort of dependency, or feelings of being incomplete, all these desires need to be dealt with before a marriage, so they don't backfire on you. It's important to get wise counsel before making a lifetime commitment. Wait upon the Lord and He will guide you in the right direction in all you do.

The same way that gold and silver are refined by fire, the Lord purifies your heart by tests and trials of life, (Proverbs 17:3, TPT).

Let us pray: *Lord I give my life to you. Have your way with every decision that is required in my life. I lay all decisions at your feet. Help me to wait upon you and not take matters into my own hands when I feel inpatient. My life is in your hands; your Word says, "I will instruct and teach you in the way which you should go; I will counsel you with my eye upon you."(Psalms 32:8, NASB). Therefore, I put my trust in you.*

CHAPTER ELEVEN

PARK AVENUE MIRACLE

Psalms 28:7 (NIV) "The Lord is my strength and my shield; my heart trusts in him, and I am helped."

One morning, before getting ready for work, I prayed my usual prayer, *Lord please protect me*. That morning I recall reading, *Isaiah 40:5 (NIV), "And the Glory of the Lord will be revealed, and all mankind together will see it. For the mouth of the Lord has spoken."*

That summer morning, I decided to wear a short sleeve dress that was bright yellow on the top and black on the bottom. All throughout the day, people at work were looking at me strangely. My thoughts were, I'll never wear this dress again – it's probably too bright.

Heading home after work, I was praying in the spirit along Park Avenue and then headed toward Second Avenue. All of a sudden, it felt like my feet were not touching the sidewalk. Then, as I was walking, I sensed a transparent tube coming down from above and over me. It felt so good whatever it was. I shortly reached Second Avenue and a homeless person was looking at me from a distance. As I approached him, he jumped off the cement wall that he was sitting on and attacked me. He lunged for my throat with his two hands raised but, trying to press through to reach me, he could not penetrate this invisible shield around me. I froze in the moment as I watched him try to press through. Then slowly lifting up my right hand with finger pointed at him, I said, "Jesus, Jesus, Jesus." On the third "Jesus" he fell backward on the sidewalk, and I was able to escape. Within minutes I reached home. I was shaken up but when I got inside my apartment, my Bible was still open to *Isaiah 40:5* from the morning. It read, *"And the glory of the Lord shall be revealed, and all flesh shall see it together: for the mouth of the Lord hath spoken it."*

I knew then why people were looking at me strangely at work. It wasn't the yellow dress I wore. It was from praying so much and calling out to God for protection, that the glory was all over me throughout the day. I must have appeared to look like a light bulb shining in the dark.

From that time forward, I knew that God was my protection and will always shield me from all harm. He revealed Himself by Name, Jehovah Roi, my Protector. As you walk with the Lord, He will protect you. He is your shield in times of trouble.

The next morning, I took the subway to Times Square Church, Sunday service. While sitting in my seat, I heard the Lord say in my spirit, "Get up from your knees, no more tears, move forward." And that's exactly what I did. Just hearing His voice strengthened me to leap forward knowing the love of God and the plans He had for my life.

I had been crying out to God for restoration, for deliverance from all that wasn't pleasing to Him, and asking Him to rescue me from myself. God answered my prayer by giving me a revelation concerning praise and worship. *It was through praise and worship that God saved, healed, and delivered me.* Through praise and worship, you get to know the Lord by His great Name and exchange what you are with who He is. Know that you are loved by our Heavenly Father.

> *Psalms 139:15,16 (NIV) says, "My frame was not hidden from you when I was made in the secret place. When I was woven together in the depths of the earth, your eyes saw my unformed body. All the days ordained for me were written in Your book before one of them came to be."*

Receive His love; that's what He wants you to do. He has a wonderful plan for your life. It's written in your book in Heaven. Chapter by chapter all the days ordained for you were written before one of them came to be. *"How precious are your thoughts to me, O God" (verse 17)*! You're in His every thought! What an awesome God we serve!

ENCOUNTERS WITH GOD

Pain changes you. Pain brings you closer to God. I know a name that is greater than your pain. That Name is Jesus, the author and finisher of your faith. Pain motivates you to move forward in all that He has called you to do. Pain makes you a threshing sledge in the spirit to take authority over demon spirits that come to harass you in your mind and every area of your life. When we go through hardships, it often prepares ordinary people for an awesome destiny and future.

The time is now where we see an increase in His presence. The time is now when all flesh together shall see the revelation of the glory of God. It's in these days that God is coming to us to reveal Himself and His power. In John 11:40 (NIV), Jesus said, "*Did I not tell you that if you believed, you would see the glory of God?*" God wants us to desire in our heart to see His Glory manifested and to know His voice.

My prayer for you is to receive His love now -- take a deep breath -- breathe in the breath of life. Breathe His love into your soul, your mind and spirit. Now pause, allow His love to saturate your innermost being. God made you because He loves you and desires to shower His love upon you!

CHAPTER TWELVE

GOD REDEEMS THE TIME

Joel 2:25 (NASB) "Then I will make up to you for the years that the swarming locust has eaten..."

I met with Sister Gwen and told her I was thinking about going to college. With her blessings, I started to search out a college program for working adults. Walking by the spirit, I took a class at City College and after a few semesters, I applied to Marymount Manhattan College and got accepted. That was a miracle in itself to be able to transfer my credits. At Marymount College, I attended classes at night since I had a full-time job.

The first year at Marymount, I was able to apply all the years of dramatic arts training as life experience credits toward my B.A. degree in English Literature. Graduating was a supernatural event because I flew through college within a short period of time. He redeemed the time that the *"locust had eaten."*

He did it all! When you follow the Lord, He will order

your steps. You first need to take a step forward and watch Him open the doors. Be fearless and take the step forward. It's only by the grace of God that you can accomplish so much through Him. There are no limitations in Him! We are to trust and obey what the Spirit of the Lord is saying and take that step and leap forward.

I furthered my education and received an M.A. degree from Teachers College, Columbia University, NYC, and thereafter a Ph.D. in Religious Studies at Tabernacle Bible College and Seminary, Tampa, Florida. All this course work was accomplished part-time. It was the Lord who gave me the discipline, perseverance, and funding to accomplish all that He wanted to do as I was thrust into the Business sphere of influence.

God will do the same for you -- All you need to do is ask and He will fulfill the desires of your heart. He will thrust you forward as you take that first step.

A LIMITLESS GOD

Our God reigns with limitless possibilities for your life. As you follow Christ, He will open doors that no man can shut. He is a God that already planned your life's destiny. It is written in Psalms 139:16 (TPT), *"You saw who you created me to be before I became me!"*

As carriers of the glory, we are entering into the greatest days where we are seeing God display His power as protector, healer, provider, and deliverer. The Prophet Isaiah writes, *"Arise, shine, for your light has come, and the glory of the Lord rises upon you." (Isaiah 60:1, NIV).*

God's people are coming into new assignments and entering our greatest days of seeing the power of God's Names and Nature displayed. Something glorious is about to happen because he is inviting you to come up higher in Him. His glory is meant to be imparted to you so that you shine for Him and transform your sphere of influence. When you experience the limitless glory realm, you want to change and never to return to the old ways and patterns.

In Hebrews 13:8 (NIV) it says, *"Jesus Christ is the same yesterday and today and forever."* Although the testimonials and witness of the "Glory Encounters" that you've read in this book occurred in the past, God can do the same today and even more because He never changes. His glory is limitless because God is the same forever!

I pray that you will have an increase in the presence of God and come to know His glory. This is an invitation to receive the presence of God to transform your life and ministry. Are you wanting to be changed and to see His glory? I know you do. Open your heart and ask God to show you His glory presence and believe that He loves you. God designed you to live in His glory, the burning place of affection for Him.

For those who do not know the Lord, this is an invitation to receive Jesus Christ, Yeshua Hamashiach, as your personal Savior. As you open your heart and receive Him, you will sense His loving presence around you. He loves you and wants you to know Him. Won't you let Him in today?

A PROPHETIC WORD OF ENCOURAGEMENT FOR YOU

"Trust me and I will fulfill the dreams that I put inside you. You are mine and no one will snatch you out of my hand. My Spirit will go before you. I am your everlasting Father who has compassion on you. Fear not. Take your past, present and future and lay it at my feet and I will lead you with my outstretched arm in the way you should go. I am the God of your salvation, and you are in my hands, saith the Spirit of the Lord."

I INVITE YOU TO PRAY WITH ME AND TOUCH HEAVEN TOGETHER

My Father, in the Name of Jesus,

I give you my entire life so that you will be glorified through me. Do in me whatever pleases you so your Name will be exalted in the earth. I will never be satisfied with anything less than you. Mark me with the fire of your Glory. Open my senses and teach me discernment to know the Glory of God. Expand my ability to recognize you and open my spirit to allow the Hope of Glory, who lives inside me, to come forth. I was born for your Glory to become known in the earth. Your Kingdom come, your will be done, on earth as it is in heaven. Help me to walk in kingdom power displaying your Glory as you see fit, with all authority and dominion speaking forth your Word.

I surrender my life to you. Help me to seek you in everything in this life and continually change me as I stand in your glorious presence. I want to be so close to you to hear your thoughts and divine plans. I receive and accept your love. Because you loved me, I can love you back and love others.

Father, when I was created, before putting me in my mother's womb, you held me as you poured inside your plans and purpose for my life. You designed me to live in your Glory, the burning place of affection for you. Let the eternal flame of my altar never burn out. Make me a house of prayer for all nations. I want to glorify you in the earth with all that you designed me to do.

Thank you for your thoughts of me that my name is written in your Book. Help me to fulfill each chapter written about me in this life and the life to come. And, when all is finished, I long to hear the gentle voice of the Spirit say, "Well done my good and faithful servant, enter into my Kingdom."

ENDNOTES

[1] Glory, A Jerusalem Experience, Ruth Ward Heflin, Destiny Image Publishers, 1990.
[a] Ruth's Music and Words, "I Ask for the Nations," page 194.

[2] The Messianic Church Arising, Dr. Robert Heidler, Glory of Zion International, 2006

[3] Messianic fulfillment in the New Testament Gospels: John 1:1; Matthrew 8:16-17, 26:62-63, 27:12-14, 38, 57; Mark 15:27-28; Luke 23:33; Romans 4:25; 1 Corinthians 15:3.

NASB: New American Standard Bible

NIV: New International Version Bible

NLT: New Living Translation Bible

TPT: The Passion Translation Bible

ABOUT THE AUTHOR

Mary Cerciello is a Marketplace Apostle and Prophetic Intercessor. She served for several years under Apostle Mario Bramnick at New Wine Ministries Church, Cooper City, Florida, in various prayer initiatives throughout the state of Florida as well as the online World Prayer Network.

Prior to moving to South Florida, Dr. Mary also served for many years under Rev. Gwendolin Sims Warren, Breath of Life Ministries, New York City and Pastor David Wilkerson as the ministry merged with the Times Square Church.

She also served in leadership and prophetic training with Rev. Ruth Ward Heflin Ministries in Ashland, Virginia and Mt. Zion Fellowship, Jerusalem.

Dr. Mary holds a Master's Degree from Teacher's College, Columbia University, New York City, and a Doctorate in Religious Philosophy from the Tabernacle Bible College in Tampa, FL.

Dr. Mary resides in the Palm Beaches, Florida.

For speaking inquiries, please email:

Mary@allabouttheglory.com

Follow me at Facebook **@Maryallabouttheglory**

Instagram: **Mary_allabouttheglory**

Twitter: **Mary_4theglory**

SUMMARY

Touching Heaven from the Empire State Building, Glory Encounters in Heavenly Places, is about the Glory of God and how the church today can tap into heavenly encounters and experience His Glory presence. Many Christians struggle with spiritual things but with the understanding of praise and worship, you learn to enter into His glory presence and catch it. There is rest and ease in the glory to every life struggle.

God designed you to dwell in His presence because He loves you. In His presence transforms your life and enables you to walk as a carrier of His Glory, to bring heaven to earth. Through the insights in this book will enable you to –

- Understand the Glory realm, become a walking carrier with influence.
- Cease from your struggle about spiritual things, catch the principles of praise, worship, and the Glory.
- Understand the revelation of His presence, refusing to settle for substandard Christianity.
- Develop a hunger and passion for God, become a witness and experience His divine power.
- Develop a trust in God and see Him work in your life to fulfill the destiny He has for you.

CPSIA information can be obtained
at www.ICGtesting.com
Printed in the USA
LVHW030754221122
733723LV00015B/620